My Name Is Baljit But You Can Call Me Gary

The Alternative Guide To Indian Culture

by

Amit Rajp

authorHOUSE®

AuthorHouse™ UK Ltd.
500 Avebury Boulevard
Central Milton Keynes, MK9 2BE
www.authorhouse.co.uk
Phone: 08001974150

First published by AuthorHouse 1/19/2009

ISBN: 978-1-4259-9009-1 (sc)

Printed in the United States of America
Bloomington, Indiana

This book is printed on acid-free paper.

This book is dedicated to my nephew,
Aryan S.C. Mohla.

Smile.

From one cheeky monkey to another.

CONTENTS:

Acknowledgements

I would like to take this opportunity to thank
my dear sister, Sonia Mohla, for her tireless
reading, faith and guidance.

Many thanks to Amee Pandya for her
encouragement and undoubted
support of the book
from the start.

Last, but certainly by no means least,
a big 'Raah' to Naomi Jones-Owen.
I cannot thank you enough for your
smiles, sarcasm and sanity.
'This Country.'
x

"While there is tea, there is hope."
- Arthur W. Pinero.

WHY TUPPERWARE
ARE LIKE DRUGS

What is the fixation that mums, aunties, nans (*nannijis*), and grans (*bibijis*) have with plastic containers? It's like Asian women have an addiction to plastic Tupperware! The person that sets up the first 'Tupperware Addiction Clinic' for Asian women is going to make a lot of money - probably some Asian guy who will acquire a forged certificate from India.

Every Asian family has one cupboard in the kitchen that resembles a shrine to plastic Tupperware, or *dubbai*. Many Asian families even have stockpiles in the garage. Imagine that: a temple filled with every type of plastic container. I wonder if aunties take their shoes off and cover their heads as a mark of respect before entering the Tupperware temple.

Like most Tupperware (drugs), plastic-container users (otherwise affectionately known as '*dubbai* women') can exist in many addictive forms ranging from the low-level addict to the hard-core. First, the auntie who is a low-level addict (merchandise includes ice cream containers and those cheap microwaveable plastic boxes you get from the local takeaway). This is the kind of Asian woman that keeps plastic containers 'just in case'.

She happily trades containers with other low-level addicts and never complains as long as the number of containers stays the same: they can happily increase, but they can never drop! If there is a reduction in number, this can cause a lot of anxiety to the low-level addict, and often a refusal to hand out any more plastic containers can be observed by the subtle yet assertive request that fellow low-level addicts bring their own.

Now in theory this seems perfectly adequate in any other social situation. Imagine a guy hosting a party and saying to his mates, "Hey, I'm having a party; bring a bottle!" Asian women feel the same way about recycling plastic containers. I don't understand why this is such a sensitive issue. Surely, the stigma attached to this uncontrolled transit of plastic containers could be alleviated by the purchase of the occasional tub of ice cream whilst shopping or of takeaway food to replenish reduced numbers and restore *dubbai* harmony.

As an aside, the Asian woman's role in recycling plastic containers is surely single-handedly keeping the Earth eco-friendly!

The hard-core addict, however, not only uses such expendable tacky plastic containers (for friends and distant relations) but also goes out of her way to purchase specific, 'high quality' Tupperware. I call this the Boomerang Stash. This is the precious stash that goes out to people who will think highly of the hard-core addict's standards in food storage and know that it must be returned immediately after use.

They are treated like a library book; the hard-core addict will even travel great distances to collect this high quality merchandise, with specific lids that go with it. Yes, that's right: hard-core addicts don't mix and match their *dubbai*.

Shall I tell you why they buy them? Shall I? It's because they think that high quality Tupperware will never get stained with that dirty turmeric stain that sediments in the container after putting a curry in it. Indian food will stain anything and everything. Why do you never see turmeric being removed in cleaning commercials? It's because nothing on the face of this Earth can shift it!

This is a phenomenon that will never go away, and every time you empty plastic containers in your house, ready to chuck them in the bin, your mum (no matter where she is in the house, she can sense this by radar) will shout out, "Don't chuck the *dubbai* away; wash it out; we can use it – just in case."

WHY 'YOU ALWAYS COULD HAVE DONE BETTER!'

Why are Asian parents never really fully satisfied with their childrens' exam results or achievements? 'Hey, Dad, I got seven 'A' grades for my exams. What do you mean I should have got more? I could only take seven subjects!'

This is the sole reason why Asian kids are generally so bright at school: they don't know what complete achievement is. They are programmed to believe from their parents that what they achieve could and should always be improved. I bet, at one stage in your life, you have happily exclaimed to your father that you got 98% in an exam and heard this reply, 'Good. So what happened to the other 2% then?' It's really clever when you think about it.

I was never scared about my school reports. I used to judge my progress on my parents' behaviour after coming back from the parent-teacher evenings. If they told me, 'You did okay, but you can do better.' That meant my teachers thought I was grade 'A' material. If my folks came back with some maths or science textbooks (that they just happened to purchase on the way home at nine o'clock in the evening from an Indian backstreet bookshop, so I could get started immediately), this meant that I was on a grade 'B', and if my parents came home with telephone numbers of maths or science tutors, then that meant I was on a grade 'C'.

If my parents came home looking angry (because they felt ashamed of being spoken to by the teachers about how bad I was doing), then I would assume the 's*** is going to hit the fan; better get ready to listen to my new study routine,' which felt like a prisoner of war camp: no TV, no games, no smiling, and, worse still, having to show my homework to my parents when I had completed it.

How degrading was that? Now there was another person (always my dad) that I had to impress with my homework other than my teacher. Such embarrassment would often be accompanied by irony, given that my dad wouldn't have a clue about my trigonometry homework but would attempt to mark it like a maths professor anyway.

What was even more embarrassing was my dad using Vedic maths (an ancient Indian system of numerology) to show me an easier way to solve the problem whilst foraging through complex calculations on what seemed like fifteen reams of paper and still not coming up with the correct answer. In frustration, I would frequently refer to this style of learning as 'homeopathic maths'. This infuriated my dad who would then decide to discuss (two-hour history lecture) how the conception of the number zero and the decimal system arose in India. However, in hindsight, it was nice to know that he took an interest.

To be fair, I did pretty well at school, and my parents rarely resorted to the 'textbook' stage. They employed this tactic only four times during my school career: between the end of every summer term and the beginning of every autumn term (1988–1993). Seriously though, the introduction of the 'textbook' towards the end of the holidays served as an appropriate and timely reminder to not rest on one's laurels.

Asian parents never come back smiling from parent-teacher evenings. A child prodigy who has just discovered the cure for cancer will still see his or her parents come home looking like they have just witnessed a major traffic accident.

Another thing, most Asian parents never care about drama, history, geography, and art. These are called the humanities subjects (my dad called them the bulls*** subjects). Asian parents believe that the national curriculum consists solely of maths and science. You could argue that such subject specific loyalty was meant to lure you into the medical profession, but I also think it was due to the proud history of India's contributions to arithmetic and astrology.

I always thought when I was younger that those Indian people famous in the arts (such as Lata Mangeshkar or Asha Bhosle) probably had little parental influence or had some major parental tragedy that allowed them to flourish in the 'arty-farty' subjects.

My dad believed going to school was for study and nothing else. I'm sure I had a schoolboy crush but was too fixated on studying to remember! My dad always paid great attention in my schooling. I remember being selected to play for the school football team and my father saying these words, which crushed me at the age of fourteen – ironically I will probably be saying them to my son in due course: 'Do you want to be a professional footballer, or do you want to study hard at school and have a career? *Huh?*'

I hated the '*Huh*' at the end of the sentence when my dad spoke because the '*Huh*' was not meant in the sense of a question. It actually translated as 'Do not even think about answering; staying silent means you are in full agreement.'

Now you can imagine that an Asian kid surrounded by this kind of environment can only take so much, and this is where you make the biggest mistake of your young life. When you are repeatedly told by your parents that you can do better and you decide to defend yourself, you say these immortal yet haunting words: 'If achieving these grades in biology, chemistry, and maths is not good enough and I can do better, why didn't you do better in school then?'

This is where the heavens part, thunder and lightning roar, and even God surely must cover His eyes with His almighty hands as your parents slowly begin to lose their temper. You hear something like this – and it's always said by your mother.

'Your father works 27 hours a day (there are 24 hours in a day, you still want to correct her, but you decide it's probably best not to act remotely arrogant) in the factory to make sure you have the uniform, the books, and the computer at home so you can study. We had nobody supporting us when we came to this country; we didn't have these things. Nobody gave us the help you have got; we had to support the family. I was looking after ten nieces and nephews on one hip and my twelve brothers and sisters.' Your dad will then utter the 'racialism' line: 'Back in those days, people were very racialist.' (I really don't know why Asian people can't pronounce the word 'racist' or 'racism').

You look a fool; you sit and hear these words ringing in your ears over and over: 'We only want what's best for you.' Consequently, you don't sleep for the rest of the night because you feel guilty, and you go to school, work your nuts off, and that's why 'you can always do better.'

SAAG (SPINACH):
THE ONE DAY THEORY

This is something I have never managed to figure out. Ever since I was a kid, my mum would make SAAG. To emphasise and honour the importance of SAAG in Asian life, I refer to it in capital letters!

I truly believe that SAAG is one of the most crucial elements of Asian life, and, more importantly, whenever you mention the word 'SAAG' to anyone, nine times out of ten, no matter who you speak to (friends, relatives, aliens), they always say this famous line: 'SAAG always tastes better the day after.'

Funnily enough, when you read the title of this chapter, I bet the first thing that came into your head was, 'SAAG always tastes better the day after.' This is normally followed by a yearning sound that resembles 'mmmmm' or 'aaaah'.

I have always imagined what it would be like to see a 'SAAG' TV commercial break that resembles the Bisto gravy advertisements. Imagine an Asian family sitting around the dining table, a matriarchal figure serves SAAG while the children inhale deeply and longingly mutter the words 'Ah, SAAG!'

Let's make one thing clear though, when I say SAAG, I am not referring to the frozen or tinned variety – that's a definite no-no in Asian households. I don't know about you, but I saw my mum prepare at least thirteen (hundred) types of spinach. What is with that? I always thought there was only one kind of spinach leaf. (You don't see your mum cut different types of cauliflower when she is making *Aloo Gobi*, do you?)

I have always had the inclination that my mum added virtually any green-leafed vegetable if it was handy. 'Oh look, there's some green foliage hanging from a carrot; there's some leaves on the dead plant in the living room.'

I'm pretty sure my mum would have added marijuana leaves if we had it growing at home. What I found completely ironic was that in contrast to other 'less influential' Asian dishes (which were easier to prepare and typically exuded an intriguing aroma of Indian flavours), the painstaking preparation of SAAG resembled a rite of passage, which never smelt nice while it was being cooked.

The prolonged efforts of my mother slaving away in the kitchen, having virtually explored the vegetation of the local park in search of a tantalising selection of exotic leaves for the SAAG, culminated in anything but a delicious aroma, let alone the potential to strut its stuff on the palate.

It smelled just like what was literally being cooked: a bunch of green leaves with 15 kilograms of butter. This was not the most pleasant of odours, and whenever you remarked as to how bad the SAAG smelt, your mum would always shout the same line: 'How do you think they make it in the restaurants!? *Huh?* Wait till you eat it first!'

Anyway, moving on, I would sit at dinnertime and wait for the SAAG. I never could contain my excitement, although whenever I ate it on the first night, it never reached the epic proportions that I had imagined.

What's more annoying is that I still go through this same routine of emotions every time, like some 'Groundhog SAAG Day'. You would think that by now I would have figured out my emotions towards first night SAAG. However, as if by magic, little SAAG pixies playfully appeared in my mum's SAAG pot overnight and transformed it into the most amazing dish that ever existed.

It tasted so good that even if God had given Adam a choice between the apple and second night SAAG, then throughout the history of time the phrase 'A dish of SAAG a day keeps the doctor away' would not seem so crazy after all. However, it wouldn't surprise me if some Asians somewhere believed the theory 'Got a headache, *betaa* (son)? Go eat some SAAG. Got a bruise, *beti* (daughter)? Rub some SAAG on it.'

I still can't figure out why SAAG tastes so good the next day. Maybe even the great Albert Einstein got stuck trying to work it out. Surely he must have had SAAG in his lifetime because it's good for your brain. (Well, that's what my mum tells me.) I have worked as a research scientist trying to find clues to cure cancer, yet nothing on this planet would give me greater satisfaction than someone explaining to me why SAAG tastes so good after the first day.

SPEAKING ENGLISH

I have never understood why Asian people give themselves English names that are nowhere near linked to their own. 'My name is Baljit, but everybody calls me Gary.' Who decides on these names? Is it by non-Asians that can't pronounce the name 'Baljit', or is there a new pseudo religion called 'Indoenglish.' where Asians with unpronounceable names get baptised in a font of Indian cooking oil and given a surreal English alternative?

Even when Asians use English-sounding names similar to their own, these names are so unpopular that you have neither met an English person with that name in your entire life, nor will you (names such as Kishan to Keith and Raj to Roger). What I have always pondered is why are Asians just using English names? Why not African names? Imagine the same setting, 'My name is Baljit, but everybody calls me Umbaffa.'

I think Asians do this to make life easier for English people who always seem to mispronounce and mess up their names. How difficult is it? I can't possibly imagine an English guy saying 'Bal—, b—, erm is it alright if I call you Dave? We have another Asian guy called Dave on the shop floor. We can call him Dave One and you Dave Two. Sorted!'

I love listening to first generation Asian relatives speak in English. Everyone has relatives who use singular terms instead of plural and vice versa. Imagine an uncle asking his two kids before ordering drinks at a restaurant, 'Hey, Bunti, you want Cokes? Moona, you want Cokes? That's two Coke thanks.'

What really gets me going is when Asian people 'Asianise' everyday English vocabulary. I always thought my uncle referred to IKEA (pronounced 'ee-kee-aa') as a country in the Indian subcontinent where you could purchase a wide range of flat-pack wooden furniture at affordable prices. Our beloved 'racialism/racialist' example rears its ugly head yet again. I still can't figure that one out.

Nothing beats the many phrases that Asian men say to describe how well they are doing. A Ravi Shankar–like upward wrist movement normally accompanies these phrases: 'first-class', 'tip-top', and 'set'. Classic or what?

Funnily enough, why can't Asians pronounce words beginning with the letter 'Y'? Common words include 'yeah' (pronounced as 'jeh') and 'you' (pronounced as 'juu'). What's all that about? The translated word 'jungesters' for 'youngsters' is my favourite.

Some Asians originating from East Africa can't pronounce any word which comprises the letter 'V'? I don't understand! To see if you are one of these Asians, read out the sentence below:

'Vol au Vents are vivacious, voluptuously velvet and very vibrant said Venkatesh Vivavarty whilst driving his Volkswagen.'

OBJECTION, MILORD!

Why the funny title you may ask? In a court scene, which is almost always at the beginning of a Bollywood movie, you will hear the dialogue 'Objection, Milord!' If it's said by the hero or his lawyer, it will always be overruled, otherwise it will be sustained.

To be honest, I'm not a big fan of Bollywood movies nowadays. They just seem to be tacky imitations of dire Hollywood films that came out the year before. How often do you hear Steven Spielberg directing a film based on the inspiration of *Devdas* or any other Bollywood movie?

Maybe I am being a bit too harsh. Some recent Bollywood movies are worth their weight in gold, but I can't help comparing them to the 'old school' Bollywood classics. These were sensational movies with amazing songs.

'The Godfather' trilogy of Bollywood movies if you will: *Sholay*, *Silsila*, and *Kabhi Kabhi* (timeless movies of epic proportions); the 'Goodfellas' style movie *Jaanbaaz* (drugs, extortion, and betrayal); and the 'Saturday Night Fever' style movie *Disco Dancer* (Mithun was the main man. *Jimmy Jimmy. Aaja!*).

What's amazing about these classic 'films' (otherwise affectionately known as 'filums' by Asians; East African Asians prefer to use the term 'mooowie') is that similar to Bollywood movies today, where you could work out the plot within the first five minutes of the film, there was a sense of nostalgia and panache that you just don't see anymore. The songs were amazing, timeless symphonies that couples still use at Asian weddings for their first dance.

I love what non-Asian people say when they pass comments about Bollywood movies. The compliments are always the same: 'It's so colourful, isn't it? There are a lot of songs aren't there? The actresses are very pretty, aren't they? They speak such good English as well!' It's as if they are too embarrassed to ask the glaringly obvious questions that Asian people unquestionably accept when watching Bollywood movies time and time again. This is not blissful ignorance. Asians are certainly not afraid to poke fun at themselves publicly (on the Web) about these bizarre 'Bollywood mysteries'.

Why does it take four hours for the hero and the heroine to fall in, out, and back in love again? How come the blind paraplegic mother of the hero suddenly defies medical science by regaining her sight and physical attributes in the family reunion scene at the end?

Why is it that the hero will show no pain whilst taking the most awful beating but will wince in agony when the heroine tries to clean his wounds with a tissue? Nothing is too tight for Madhuri? Sorry, that's a personal one.

Why does the hero wait patiently for his heavily outnumbered enemies laden with hockey sticks to attack him one by one during a fight scene?

Why is it that two brothers separated in childhood will always grow up on opposite sides of the law, with the wayward sibling suddenly turning over a new leaf, but not before beating up the true villain and being pardoned for all his sins in the family reunion finale?

Enough is enough; however, the list is truly endless. I will tell you what I personally never figured out when

I was a kid and probably never will. I never understood the kiss/no kiss, which turns into the noserub, cheek to cheek embrace that happens between the hero and heroine at the end of a romantic scene or song.

I always used to joke about these supposedly romantic moments to family: since when did we turn into Eskimos, rubbing noses when feeling amorous? You can always look on the bright side of Bollywood!

The one Indian epic where you couldn't joke harmlessly about the acting style was the televised portrayal of the Indian epic, the *Mahabharat*. I remember flippantly saying to my mum early one Saturday morning when I was a kid (I never understood why they would show the *Mahabharat* at half past four in the morning), that one of the actors portraying a symbolic character wasn't very convincing.

My mum gave me such a telling off for this alleged mockery of acting prowess. The sheer audacity of such criticism apparently meant that I was ridiculing Hinduism and no longer believing in God. You can joke about bad acting in Bollywood, but joke about bad acting in the *Mahabharat*? Bad move!

RAKSHA BANDHAN (BROTHER-SISTER DAY)

Now I'm going to try to be fair and give a well-judged opinion on Raksha Bandhan. For those not in the know, Raksha Bandhan is a Hindu festival that celebrates the relationship between brothers and sisters.

A loving exchange whereby a sister ties a *rakhi* (cotton thread) around her brother's wrist symbolising the circle of love that she will provide throughout his life and beyond, whilst in return, the brother gives his caring, loving sister a ridiculously ludicrous amount of money that has just been sanctioned by the Chancellor of the Exchequer and the Bank of England.

Okay, give me a break! I tried to be fair. I can't help starting off all spiritual about Raksha Bandhan when I talk about the sister part, but I always feel bittersweet about the brother's bit. Even now, at the grand old age of thirty-one. You can't help being biased in your view on Raksha Bandhan. Now please don't get me wrong here, I am not knocking the symbolism. I think it's beautiful; I really do.

Even when I was a kid, who never had (let alone appreciated) money of my own, whenever my mum gave me twenty-one pounds from her purse to give directly to my sister after she tied a thread that resembled an eighties Casio digital calculator watch with what seemed a genetically engineered oversized lotus flower (symbol of purity) as a substitute – I'll come onto that in a minute – I always thought I was getting the raw deal.

As the years continued and I started to earn money of my own, it still seemed really unfair, and not just because I obviously gave considerably more money. (Asian men have little choice in becoming 'annual high-rate Raksha Bandhan taxpayers').

I'm sure the Chancellor of the Exchequer mentions it in his budget speech. 'Madam Speaker, Asian men are not only subjected to the annual governmental tax regulations every April, they also qualify unconditionally for the age-related incremental "Raksha Bandhan Tax" (which is set at no less than fifty-one pounds). This tax is also upheld in favour of any female relatives and friends that display sisterlike qualities. Bankruptcy declaration documents can be completed in such cases.'

I love that, don't you: eleven pounds, twenty-one pounds, fifty-one pounds, one hundred and one pounds? What is with Asian people when they give money gifts? It has to be these lucky numbers. Anyway, I'm going off track. Where was I? Oh yeah, my sister always seemed to gain the greatest satisfaction and the biggest Colgate smile when I handed the cash over.

It's as if she wanted to get the symbolism over as quickly as possible. It's got to the point now, that at the age of thirty-one, she just asks for my bank account number so she can siphon off her fee from my account directly.

My sister used to get such a kick about the religious stuff when she was younger. She would apply the biggest *tilak* (red dot of vermillion powder) on my forehead (symbolic of Hindu worship), so I looked like a priest from a Bollywood film. Ironically, only on this day, my sister would turn into such a religious nut. She took great pleasure in my embarrassment and would constantly threaten to tell my mum if I ever tried to wipe my brow because I felt uncomfortable resembling a kamikaze target in a bullfighting arena.

It's as if all men are programmed that on Raksha Bandhan they must accept a large red bullseye dot on their foreheads, be force-fed an Indian sweet that they hate, and have a bloody huge multi-coloured thread (which I didn't mind) with a huge lotus flower the size of Peru (which I bloody did mind), all of this administered by a sarcastic sister, and guess what? She is given money for it.

Asian men are extremely astute in economics, business, and finance. I think it's quite ironic that on this day, all sense of value goes out of the window. Girls, you know you love it. Hey, it's cool to admit it.

This is the most bittersweet thing about Raksha Bandhan for me: there are some girls out there that look beyond the financial gain and unselfishly say this (like a Bollywood film actress): 'Dearest brother, I don't want any money. I just want you to live a long life filled with peace and happiness.'

In theory, this sounds great, but trust me dear Asian brother, you will still pay out because first, you will always fall for the reverse psychology, and second, even if you decide not to pay, your mum will kick your ass and tell you to cough up. You can't win! Although you know that deep down you love your sister for it.

I just want to admit something now (this is really for my sister, Sonia). I am not proud of this, but when I was young, I used to rip off the lotus flower of my *rakhi*. I couldn't wait to rip it off; I would even try to do it discreetly and then gasp, 'Oh no, my lotus root has come off!' A lot of boys at my school used to do the same because nobody non-Asian understood why we had what resembled a cauliflower on our wrists. By the beard of Zeus, I'm sorry.

UFOS
(UNCLE FULL OF S***)
THEORY

I don't care what you think, almost every Asian has an uncle who has been everywhere and done everything. What's more annoying is that when you were young, you were too naïve to discriminate between outright bulls*** and reality.

I heard no tales of space travel or fighter pilot action. However, what was frustrating when I was old enough to realise was that the stories were a lot more realistic and always seemed to be coincidentally linked to what I was really into as a young boy.

I would listen intently as my uncle 'told me so it must be true' that he had a Porsche and BMW (with a Lamborghini for the weekend), an eight-bedroom mansion, and contacts with really famous people I liked or even cared to mention.

I thought it was so amazing that my uncle was so humble because he managed to conceal his wealthy, luxurious lifestyle by driving a 1985 Vauxhall Cavalier whilst living in a three-bed semi-detached house in suburban Southall.

Even at an age when you were still gullible to believe Uncle's stories, you would still go out of your way to brag and even defend your uncle's tales of fame and fortune to your mates. If you were unlucky enough to have had more than one uncle who boasted such extravagant wealth and celebrity status, you would simply display all the loyalty of a Labrador at a children's party; whoever dropped the biggest crumbs of grandeur would have you at his feet.

It's pretty clear why this theory exists: macho pride. Imagine the setting:

Naïve nephew: I love Porsches; they are wicked cars! Uncle, have you got a Porsche?

Uncle: Yes, I have had one. I just sold it and bought a Vauxhall Cavalier because I'm looking for a Lamborghini Countach.

Naïve nephew: Wow! Uncle, you're the best.

Now please don't think I'm being sexist here, but your average auntie was more interested in pinching your cheeks and force-feeding Indian sweets into your mouth when you were young.

I think exaggerated masculine pride has much to answer for. Do you know what the biggest kick in the teeth is? If you are a guy fortunate enough to become an uncle, you will end up doing exactly the same thing.

SHELL SUITS

I am, unfortunately, old enough to not only remember owning, but also wearing, a turquoise shell suit. For those of you that are fortunate (or young) enough to not know what shell suits are, then consider yourself very lucky. Shell suits were one of the 'must have' fashion items amongst Asian people in the mid-eighties. What made them more popular was that the whole family could wear them!

What I always found fascinating about shell suits was that whenever it got windy, your shell suit would always manage to double up conveniently as a parachute that speeded you along your journey. What annoyed me though was that no matter how slow you walked, one shell suit leg would ruck up, exposing your white towel sock (or almost white because your mum would put it in the washing machine with her pink sari).

Let's not make any mistakes here: there was a 'shell suit etiquette' amongst the teenagers when I was young. It seemed that the shell suit only existed in flamboyant colours ranging from turquoise blue or shocking snot green to menstrual pink, and you always, *always* wore white socks with white trainers.

Shell suits were for everyone: even your gran had probably worn a shell suit jacket at some point. What made shell suits such a fashion faux pas was the obliteration of these unwritten rules.

Why, oh why, did there always seem to be an uncle in your family who insisted on wearing his bright green shell suit with shoes? I could not imagine a more embarrassing combination than Oxford Brogues with elasticized, aquamarine shell suit bottoms.

The shell suit and flip-flop combination was also just as common, although I have a theory that most Asians would wear flip-flops with almost anything given half a chance (tuxedos, space suits, etc). Asians surely must be proud to have contributed to the number one fashion crime of the century! Give it a few years, and those light, bright, and nasty nylon waterproofs will be making a comeback.

DAD 'COSBY SHOW' MOMENTS

Now a lot of you must remember 'The Cosby Show'. It was a big, eighties family comedy about a middle/upper class African-American family going through various trials and tribulations. Each episode had a moral that was given by the star of the show, Bill Cosby (who played Dr. Cliff Huxtable).

To be fair, when you saw Dr. Cliff Huxtable, he seemed like the perfect dad: he was cool, he was funny, he had a good relationship with his kids, and he managed to guide his children in a really cool way by giving them 'moral stories'. This was a lot different from the grief I got from Mom and, God forbid, 'The Look' from Dad.

Whenever you watch these 'my children are out of control' TV shows now, you always see this good cop/

bad cop theory of parenting: the mum is the soft and gentle parent, and the father represents the stern, resilient counterpart. When I was a kid, there was no good cop/ bad cop. It was bad cop (Mum) and FBI/CIA/ Royal Marine Paratrooper (Dad). That's why you rarely see an Asian kid on these programmes.

I don't know about you, but when I was a kid (no, not when I was twenty-five) out with my mum and I was being rude or silly in public, she never had a problem giving me a polite slap. The sheer embarrassment of looking a complete and utter fool in public made me never ever attempt a silly stunt again.

I used to love seeing my mum managing to smile at me whilst gritting her teeth and muttering 'Just you wait 'til I get you home' whenever I was being a fool at someone else's house. She never failed to assert her authority when I played up; even in the car, she would manage to wrap her arms around her seat and cheekily pinch my calves when I was picking on my sister.

My dad only had to give me 'The Look' whenever my mum felt that her powers of teaching me a lesson had waned. I used to shudder at the thought of 'The Look'. Fortunately, as I got older, my dad started to adopt the

'Dr. Cliff Huxtable' approach, and although I never really appreciated it at the time, for some strange reason unbeknown to me, his moral sermons now stick to me like glue.

The one I remember most is when I had started university locally, and although still living at home, I partied hard and stayed out virtually every other night of the week. I neglected my household chores and started to treat my home as a hotel (which was quite pants really, as in most other hotels you don't get slapped across the back of your head for not cleaning your room).

It got to the point where my dad sat me down and said these immortal words: "Even the dirtiest dogs who travel everywhere throughout the day still go back to sleep at the same place every night, and even they make sure they don't sleep in a s*** hole." What did I do? I did the honourable thing and went out with the lads all night, got smashed, and stayed out for a repetition of drunken debauchery. The stupidity of youth!

When I was younger, I couldn't wait for my dad's sermons/philosophies to end (to be honest, 'The Look' didn't seem so bad), but now I can't help passing them off as my own. As I get older, I end up trying to be

Dr. Cliff Huxtable/my dad and pass on these golden nuggets of wisdom at any opportunity. Although I don't think I'm getting the message across correctly, let alone to the right age range. 'Listen, Sonny. I know you are four years old, but don't do drugs, and don't sleep like a dog okay?'

MERRY CHRISTMAS

Now I don't know about you, but when I was a kid, I used to try really hard to get the Christmas presents I always wanted. In hindsight, I was overly optimistic in my choices: battery-operated Ferrari replica car, £150 Reebok trainers. I would even go out of my way to circle items in the Argos catalogue and leave it page open so my mum and dad would get the hint.

Most non-Asian kids at my school always got cool Christmas presents: radio-controlled cars, fifteen computer games for each of their Sega, Nintendo, and PlayStation consoles. I would have been happy with just one console and one game; I can still hear my dad bellowing in the background: 'You will not keep up your studies playing bloody toot toot games!'

To be fair, my dad did buy me a Sinclair Spectrum ZX 128. (128K! That was the bee's knees in those days, but I probably have more memory in my left testicle). I can't believe how many hours of my life I wasted trying to input programming codes to play a stunted version of Spectrum Ping Pong.

My dad had no reservations in telling me that Father Christmas didn't exist and that all presents were paid for by his and my mum's hard-earned wages. Asian kids' Christmas presents when I was young were not terribly exciting or spontaneous: new school trousers, stationery, and school bag, things that were essentials but not desirables.

It must be said that I appreciated what they did for me, and a lot of Asian kids in my school were treated the same. I used to love getting money from relatives at Christmas. Why is it that Asian kids (okay, just me) would always look at their mum or dad first before accepting any money from relatives? Your mum would then nod accordingly after the 'three-no rule,' while you are just aching to take the cash. (The 'three-no rule' refers to the number of times that Asian people refuse cash gifts by different phrases or gestures before finally accepting.)

Most relatives would give eleven or twenty-one pounds, and for the period up until you got home, you would be under the impression that the money given to you by your auntie, sanctioned by your mother, is yours. Yeah right! I would have to give the twenty-one pounds to my mum, and it would pay for some Indian sweets or a quick bite on the way home. Great! That's probably why Asian people are so good at business: they realise the value of money after parting with it begrudgingly at such an early age.

Funnily enough, when our non-Asian family friends would give me some money for Christmas, my mum would never take the money off me. To be fair, the most I would get was fifty pence for some sweets. It's like my mum was 'The Godfather' or Al Capone. She had a good racket going. I can't wait to do the same to my kids.

THE CLAIM TO FAME THEORY

Here is an experiment for you: go for a leisurely drive in your car, and whenever you see an Asian person (particularly someone who isn't related to you), preferably over thirty-five, sound your horn and acknowledge them with a wave.

I guarantee that 99.9% of the time they will wave smilingly back at you, and the mother of all ironies is that they will kid themselves, and others, that they actually know who you are. What's all that about? Asians like networking with other people. Even if they don't know them, they will know someone who does. Asian people love what I call the Claim to Fame theory.

We have a unique, inborn talent to pretend that we know people in high society as if they are our next-door neighbours. We see it as competition.

Asian women tend to compete with each other by not advertising themselves but, rather selflessly, their children's academic achievements and impressive circle of influential friends in an attempt to climb up the social ladder. Asian men are a lot more forthcoming in claiming bragging rights. You always hear two Asian men, when talking about someone they both know (or most probably don't), trying to outbid each other to be the more prominent male.

There are a couple of levels to this: The first is the 'Oh I know him very well. We go back a long way' line. This is not too invasive with a slight hint of self-righteousness, although even this simple introductory statement can lead to other Asian men proudly declaring their (longer) duration of friendship, similar to a no-limits poker game with Asian males raising the stakes (number of years) around the table.

Asian men then take it a little too far. Not only do we want to show that we know certain people very well, we can't wait to steer the conversation so that we can spout our alleged boasts at the earliest opportunity. We have to add 'The Godfather' ingredient to it because it makes us feel good and makes those listening feel insecure. 'Oh yeah, we know them very well, their family has asked us to help them many times. I sorted out their multi-storey extension in their garden.'

Then the last level is the family connection. This 'Royal Flush' of bragging rights denotes a degree of boastfulness that cannot be beaten. 'Oh yeah, Prince William's hairdresser is our second cousin's brother's auntie's great granddaughter.'

Given that Asian men are not blood-related to everyone in the entire world, Asian men often refer to the lesser ranking 'Straight Flush' of association, which indicates that they know and treat the alleged person as a family member and vice versa. 'Oh yeah, Prince William's hairdresser is like a nephew to me. He calls me Uncle all the time.'

For the love of God! How far back do people want to take it? The next time I get embroiled in a conversation similar to this with another Asian guy (an everyday occurrence), I am just going to take my apparent pseudo relationship back as far as stupidly possible: 'Oh yeah, I know Laila Rouass very well. We were embryos together. I helped sort out her multi-storey extension, and she knows me so well that she calls me Mickey, which is my family nickname.' Top that!

INDIAN EXTENSIONS
= BULK SHOPPING

I love that, don't you? Asians love to extend their houses: if you can't build out in the garden, then you can build up! We can build anything: the Taj Mahal, the Agra Fort, and Auntie's multi-storey complex in her three-foot square garden. Genius!

I have found that when non-Asian builders, who possess the necessary qualifications and craftsmanship, are offered a job in which they have no expertise, they are honest enough to say, 'Sorry, I am not experienced enough to do this job. I am not a plasterer by trade, but I can recommend someone for you.' Not like Asian builders, oh no! They never refuse any job, especially ones they can't do. They can do everything: master of all trades, plastering, moving houses to the left,

Michelangelo paintings on the ceiling. 'No problem, tip-top.'

I have yet to meet an Asian builder who has turned down work despite lacking the relevant skills required to undertake it. I will say this though, Asian builders are good at building storage rooms, and we Asians love our storage don't we? I know the reason for this: it's because we can't resist a bargain when we go shopping.

We love to stock up 'just in case'. Bulk shopping is a big Asian thing; we don't go to a local convenience store to buy weekly groceries, the odd bottle of pop, or bread and milk. We make a weekly (monthly) trip to a trade warehouse and buy bulk. I'm talking 128,000 cans of pop and 30,000 toilet rolls because in the long run it makes more sense because they will 'always come in handy!'

Whenever I used to go food shopping with my mum, all I would hear were the words 'Baked beans, pick up twelve tins. Tomato ketchup, get the 35 litre bottle.' Asian people love to supersize and bulk shop. We are so skilled in picking out bargains that it's no surprise that we are the cornerstone of the nation's shopkeepers.

You can tell when you are in an Indian convenience store because the price is made up at the till, and more importantly, we don't do 'buy one get one free'. Our comparison is 'buy a crate of 72 baked bean tins, get 1 tin free'. I have this fixation with baked beans, don't I? Probably because I have got 350 tins stored under my bed.

FASHION AND TRAVEL

Asian people love to travel, don't they? Asians love to travel so much that they only go to six places in the world. Talk about getting a wide variety of culture! I'm talking 'Pindh', which qualifies as homeland India or Pakistan; 'Caneeda' (Canada; more specifically 'Trrronto' and 'Wancoower'); 'Amriikaa' (America); 'Dhubbay' (Dubai); 'Mombasaa' (Mombasa); and of course 'Englaand,' or otherwise commonly known as 'JU K!'

You can understand why there are no travel shows on Indian TV channels because the series would only have six episodes in it. This geographical association can be explained by an important foundation of Asian culture: family life. We all know how globally extensive Asian families can be. Asians love nothing more than (or have little choice in) spending their vacation visiting family abroad due to the numerous functions that they must attend to maintain and support family togetherness (and, more importantly, avoid family politics) as well as the opportunity to reclaim unreturned Tupperware.

I love the fact that Asian people go way over the baggage limit when checking in at an airport. You always have the Asian dad who will look for and wait to have a chat with the one Asian guy or girl at the check-in desk to 'smooth things over' in accepting a luggage weight that resembles the size of a pregnant African elephant – with triplets.

I'm sure Asian people even look out for Asian check-in receptionists even on the non-Asian airlines like Air Norway or Air Scandinavia. They always think that the Indian check-in guy or girl will completely forego all sense of flight safety to ensure that Auntie's seventy-five piece Tupperware dinner set, that has been carefully smuggled within the luggage, can reach its destination.

What is with that? Why do Asians transit large supplies of Tupperware (drugs) when visiting family abroad, especially those living in vastly developed countries? I don't really understand that. Do you? You can imagine watching on CNN: 'Following that awful tragedy in

South America, we now move to the increasing crisis of the shortage of microwaveable Tupperware in Toronto.'

Another thing I still don't understand is why, for the love of God, do elderly relatives visiting from abroad always buy ill-fitting clothes as presents and then make you try them on as soon as they give it to you?

I could be wearing a space suit, ready to embark on a novel, intergalactic, exploratory trip into outer space, but that wouldn't stop my auntie trying to dress me in a one-size-fits-all bizarre hybrid of an anorak, a blouse, and a tent feebly disguised as a jumper.

The garment will look nothing short of a dress, whilst my auntie and my mum will ensure, or 'grantee' (that's an Indian guarantee by the way), that I wear this garment at the next possible outing, which is always when you bump into everyone in your social circle, including every girl that you have ever wanted to impress, leaving you cringing with embarrassment.

The token item of clothing that all men get though is the 24-inch collar white shirt (that fits nobody) with awful, multicoloured parallel stripes, that has been wrapped in cellophane since 1973.

I'm sure that these shirts have lasted since the dawn of time. I bet Eve gave Adam one when he had to cover up: a tacky white shirt wrapped in cellophane, and it's still going around. Asian women collect these shirts and recycle them around at any function.

I'm sure my dad recognised a shirt given to him last week, which was the same as the one he was given at his wedding thirty odd years ago. Now I understand the origins of the phrase 'fashion goes full circle'. It all stems from the tacky, elephant-sized, 24-inch collar white shirt wrapped in cheap cellophane.

SHAADI (MARRIAGE)

Now I am not going to critically analyse Asian matrimony: arranged marriages, caste systems, subcaste systems, super subcaste systems, dowries, and people not being with one another because they don't have the same blood group. The one thing that I have figured out from writing this book is that Asian people have a lot more in common with each other than we think. My apparent fear of being drawn into sharing my thoughts on Asian matrimony is slowly disappearing. Bear with me.

I believe, somewhat ironically, that love and marriage are already far too complicated without Asian people making it even more seriously complex. So many strive, or feel under huge pressure, to find the right caste, blood group, and chromosome number in a partner – I haven't even included those 'minor' things like attraction and personality – as well as the single quality that Asian people live, breathe, and base all judgements in life upon. The 'R' word: Respect.

Self-respect and family respect are the fabric of Asian life. We would happily cut off our nose to spite our face for it, let alone family members. Asian families and the Mafia are so similar. We only truly unite at weddings and funerals. I am sure that's probably why we love 'The Godfather' movies so much. Surely 'Respect' (in a positive way - or as my dad calls it: 'having a clean heart') in ourselves and in our prospective partners is all we and our families should strive for.

Have you ever explained to a non-Asian person the caste system and marriage? I love seeing the confused look on his or her face. It's not like they don't understand. They do have experience with this kind of thing (Catholic/Protestant, etc), but even non-Asians marvel at the level of complexity we create. When it comes to the subject of marriage, nobody does 'complicated' better than Asians.

Okay, serious thought's over. To illustrate my light-hearted approach, I thought I would show you how I described myself* on an Asian Internet matrimonial site. I haven't received any replies yet. I get the feeling that prospective ladies aren't taking my profile seriously. To be fair, having a profile name of 'dr_spankmonkey' doesn't help. You have to give me credit for originality:

I am a dynamic figure, often seen scaling walls and crushing ice. I have been known to remodel chocolate on my lunch breaks, making it more efficient in the areas of heat retention. I translate ethnic slurs for Cuban refugees; I write award-winning operas. I manage time efficiently. I woo women with my sensuous and divine tabla playing; I am an expert in Salsa, a veteran in love, and an outlaw in Southall.

Using only a stick and a large glass of water, I once single-handedly defended a small village in the Amazon Basin from a horde of ferocious army ants. I play the saxophone; I was once scouted by Manchester United.

I am the subject of numerous documentaries. When I am bored, I build large clay oven tandoors in my yard. I enjoy urban samosa filling. On Wednesdays, after work, I repair electrical appliances free of charge. I am an abstract artist, a concrete analyst, and a ruthless bookie.

Critics worldwide swoon over my original line of corduroy evening wear. I do not perspire. I am a private citizen, yet I receive fan mail. My deft floral arrangements have earned me fame in international botany circles. Children trust me. I can hurl hockey sticks at small moving objects with deadly accuracy.

I once read Paradise Lost, Moby Dick, and David Copperfield in one day and still had time to refurbish an entire dining room that evening. I know the exact location of every food item in the supermarket.

I have performed several covert operations with the CIA. I sleep once a week; when I do sleep, I sleep in a chair. While on vacation in Canada, I successfully negotiated with a group of terrorists who had seized a small kebab shop.

The laws of physics do not apply to me. I balance, I weave, I dodge, I frolic, and my bills are all paid. On weekends, to let off steam, I participate in full contact Nintendo. Years ago I discovered the meaning of life but forgot to write it down. I have played Hamlet, I have performed open-heart surgery, and I have spoken with Lata Mangeshkar. Thank you.

*Adapted from H. Gallagher: 'College Essay' (1990)

INDIAN TIMING

I have saved this 'til last, given that Indian timing is notoriously late by tradition. Asians have been consistently late since the dawn of time, which probably means about seven hours after dawn to Indians (or otherwise affectionately known as dinnertime).

British Asians have got their own internal clock, very similar to Greenwich Mean Time (GMT), called Indian Standard Time (IST). It can be calculated by a simple formula: IST = GMT + (5 minutes multiplied by the number of people).

For example, if you are waiting for two people, then add ten minutes to the time you expect them to arrive. When waiting for a coach load of 300 people (typical Asian wedding congregation), don't be surprised to meet them 1500 minutes later. This is not a hard and fast rule, but I think you get the idea!

I have patiently waited three hours for someone who told me that he was 'only five minutes away'. I get frustrated and complain that people don't keep an eye on the time, but ironically, I can't help doing the same to others no matter how hard I try to avoid being late.

Almost all Asians not only intrinsically arrive late by IST, but also hate waiting around for others who run late by IST. It's a vicious cycle, a no-win situation.

So maybe the whole lateness thing is not really our fault. What makes us unable to meet meticulous timekeeping in this way? Did God create Asians five minutes later than every other ethnic group and we have always been trying to catch up ever since?

We strive to keep appointments, meetings, and gatherings, but we never quite make it on time. Now not all Asians are like this. There are some, and remember this is a real minority, that don't arrive late to a function but appear way too early.

How many times have you arranged a party where some guests arrived much earlier than you had planned? These are the guests that are so committed to not arriving late that they turn up too early!

Do you want to know why we can't we make it on time? I'll tell you why in five minutes. I'm only five minutes away.

ABOUT THE AUTHOR

Amit Rajp is a first-time author! Arising from a research academic background at medical school as well as teaching at a prestigious grammar school in Birmingham, this is Amit's first foray into creative writing. Amit's sarcastic, raw, and down-to-earth thoughts on Indian culture are based on highlighting personal and shared experiences to which British Asian people can relate.

The Art of Happiness: Keep Smiling.
"Because of your smile, you make life more beautiful."
- Thich Nhat Hanh.

x

Lightning Source UK Ltd.
Milton Keynes UK
27 January 2010

149202UK00001B/30/P